GH00786318

DIFFICULT RIDDLES FOR SMART KIDS

400+ Difficult Riddles and Brain Teasers Your Family Will Love

Volume I

Cooper the Pooper

TABLE OF CONTENTS

INTRODUCTION

Well, hello there, young Riddler!

Welcome to what I *know* is going to be a great day.

How do I know it's going to be a great day, you might ask?

Well, you're holding something very special in your hand. In fact, you might say it's something *super* special.

See, you have a book that is filled to the brim with my best riddles — riddles that will have you guessing for days. Riddles so hard that they might melt your brain, and, of course, riddles so funny that they will have you rolling around in fits of laughter. Like I said, super special.

Believe it or not, a few years ago, I spent all my time laying in the sun, digging through the trash, chasing cats, and playing with the neighborhood kids.

But then, something happened. Things changed, and those same kids started spending all their time glued to the screen of their phones rather than play outside with *me.*

Seriously, how boring is that?

I quickly realized that something needed to change. So, I put on my thinking cap and brainstormed some great ways that kids just like you can have *real* fun with your friends and family.

And I had a brilliant idea. Yep, I started writing books — but not just any old books. They're books that are full of things you can share with people and have a whole lot of laughs while doing so — and what better way to share than with *riddles*?

I scoured the globe for the best riddles known to man. Then, I brought them together into one amazing book. These riddles have become favorites at home. My owner enjoys them, and his kids love sharing them after a long day at school. The riddles even got Aunt Mildred to smile, and she hasn't smiled since 1949.

If you are after some great riddles to share with your best friend or simply want to get your aunty to smile, I've got you covered.

Dive in and be prepared to laugh, cry, and everything in between — and if you feel your brain melting, please take a break (kidding, kidding… well, kind of.)

FOOD RIDDLES

01 What type of cheese is made backwards?

02 I'm peeled, have eyes, and I'm made into fries.
What am I?

03 Although I'm not magic,
I am a type of bean.
I'm something you can drink
That has lots of caffeine.
What am I?

04 I'm something that is white;
In a carton I am stored.
I'm something you can drink;
On cereal I am poured.
What am I?

05 What is the saddest fruit in the world?

06
I am a small round fruit,
But I'm not a lemon.
I get baked in a pie
Along with cinnamon.
What am I?

07
What's bright orange, green on top,
and sounds like a parrot?

08
What has to be broken before you can use it?

09
What kind of table is good for you to eat?

10
When does an Irish potato change its nationality?

11
In what month of the year do
people eat the least amount of food?

12

This is something yellow,
But it is not a light.
It is a citrus fruit
That's the flavor of Sprite.
What is it?

13

I'm red and have seeds;
I am also round.
Sliced up in salads
Is where I can be found.
What am I?

14

What is eaten by men, served among many, grown by many, and is white as snow?

15

What color can you eat?

16

You will buy me to eat, but you will never eat me. *What am I?*

17
A time when they are green, a time when they are brown,
But both of these times cause me to frown.
But just in between, for a very short while,
They are perfect and yellow and cause me to smile.
What are they?

18
This small, round, stone fruit
That is typically bright or dark red,
Often tops a milkshake
On a whipped cream bed.
What is it?

19
I am a seed with three letters in my name.
Take away the last two, and I still sound the same.
What am I?

20
This dish is usually eaten at breakfast
time with milk *What is it?*

21

My first is in fish but not in snails.
My second is in rabbit but not in tails.
My third is in up but not in down.
My fourth is in tiaras but not in crowns.
My fifth is in the tree you plainly see.
My whole is a food for you and me.
What am I?

22

You pick it, peel the outside, cook the inside, eat the outside, and throw away the inside.
What is it?

23

I'm a food made of flour, water, and yeast, mixed together and baked. You need me to make a sandwich. *What am I?*

24

I'm a long, green-skinned fruit with watery flesh, usually eaten raw in salads, or pickled.
What am I?

25
What water can you chew and eat?

26
I am a fruit.
If you take away my first two letters,
I am an animal.
If you take away my first and last letters,
I am a type of music.
What am I?

27
I'm a small sweet treat,
Typically round, flat, and crisp.
I come in a variety of flavors
From oatmeal raisin, to chocolate chip.
What am I?

28
I'm a pie, but I come with pepperoni and cheese.
What am I?

ANSWERS

1. Edam
2. Potato
3. Coffee
4. Milk
5. Blueberry
6. Apple
7. Carrot
8. Egg
9. A vegetable
10. When it becomes French fries
11. February (it is the shortest month)
12. Lemon
13. Tomato
14. Rice
15. Orange
16. Plate
17. Bananas
18. Cherry
19. Pea
20. Cereal
21. Fruit
22. Corn
23. Bread
24. Cucumber
25. Watermelon
26. Grape
27. Cookie
28. Pizza

ANIMAL RIDDLES

01 What always goes to bed with shoes on?

02
I am known as a king.
The jungle is where I reign.
It is hard to tame me,
And I have a large mane.
What am I?

03
I can jump, and I can climb.
With my many legs, I swing from tree to tree.
I can build a house much bigger than me.
What am I?

04
They sometimes wear a bell,
But never a rattle.
A group is known as a herd
Or sometimes as cattle.
What are they?

05 What do lazy dogs do for fun?

06

One of my favorite things
Is to run around the park.
If I am unhappy
Then you might hear me bark.
What am I?

07

I am type of animal,
But I'm not one which is furry;
I have gray skin and a long trunk
And two tusks made of ivory.
What am I?

08

If you go out on a boat
And stay there until it's late,
What is it that you might catch
With a rod, hook, and some bait?

09

What follows a dog wherever it goes?

10

What fish is in the sky at night?

11 What lives where it cannot breathe and has a hole in its back?

12 I am found in your yard, but I'm not grass.
I move slowly, but I'm not a sloth.
I have a shell, but I'm not an egg.
I have a house wherever I go.
What am I?

13 You can eat my wings,
My breast, and my legs.
Plus, when I'm alive
You can eat my eggs.
What am I?

14 Africa's where I was born.
On my head I have a horn.
What am I?

15 What jumps when it walks and sits when it stands?

16

This is something that can fly
Although it is not a kite.
It's an annoying insect
Which is small and likes to bite.
What is it?

17

I am an insect;
A hive is my home.
I eat some pollen
To make honeycombs.
I buzz and have wings,
And my tail stings.
What am I?

18

If you see this animal
And find that your paths are crossed,
Try to walk a different way
Or bad luck will be the cost.
What is it?

19

What animal would be the
best at playing video games?

20 If a car key opens a car, and a house key opens a house, then what would open a banana?

21 Agile on my feet, I drive dogs mad.
I flick my tail when I'm angry
And hum when I'm glad.
What am I?

22 The strangest creature you'll ever find:
Two eyes in the front, and many more behind.
What am I?

23 A blackbird I am similar to, but much bigger than a crow. *What am I?*

24 Always well dressed, but I never fly.
Black and white, sometimes in a tie.
I swim and slide, and I dance and glide
With one person by my side.
What am I?

25 What's black, white, and blue?

26 How do you spot a modern spider?

27 What do you call a famous lobster?

28
Its voice is like a burp,
It will swallow with a slurp,
You'll never hear it chirp.
Kiss it with a wince
And it might turn into a prince.
What is it?

29 What is a bunny's favorite music?

30 What do you call a fly with no wings?

31 What does a cat have that other animals do not have?

32 What do you call a 100-year-old ant?

33 Why are giraffes so slow to apologize?

34 I sleep by day and fly by night,
But I have no feather to aid my flight.
What am I?

35 What is as large as an elephant but has no weight?

36 How can a leopard change its spots?

37 I am an animal named after the animal I eat.
What am I?

38

I wiggle and wriggle and cannot see;
Sometimes I'm underground,
Sometimes I'm on a tree.
Sometimes I end up on a hook.
And others I can be combined with a book.
What am I?

39

Who rows quickly with four oars but never comes out from under his own roof?

40

What kind of fish chases a mouse?

41

It is a cat, but not a kitty;
You'll never catch one in a city.
Its fangs are huge, and so are its claws;
A death machine with paws and jaws.
In its own way a royal fellow,
Striped with black and clothed in yellow.
What is it?

ANSWERS

1. Horse
2. Lion
3. Spider
4. Cow
5. Chase parked cars
6. Dog
7. Elephant
8. Fish
9. Tail
10. Starfish
11. Whale
12. Snail
13. Chicken
14. Rhinoceros
15. Kangaroo
16. Mosquito
17. Bee
18. Black cat
19. Octopus
20. A monkey
21. Cat
22. Peacock

23. Raven
24. Penguin
25. A sad zebra
26. They have a website.
27. A lobSTAR
28. Frog
29. Hip-hop
30. A walk
31. Kittens
32. ANT-ique
33. It takes a long time for them to swallow their pride.
34. Bat
35. The shadow of an elephant
36. By moving from one spot to another
37. Anteater
38. Worm
39. Turtle
40. Catfish
41. Tiger

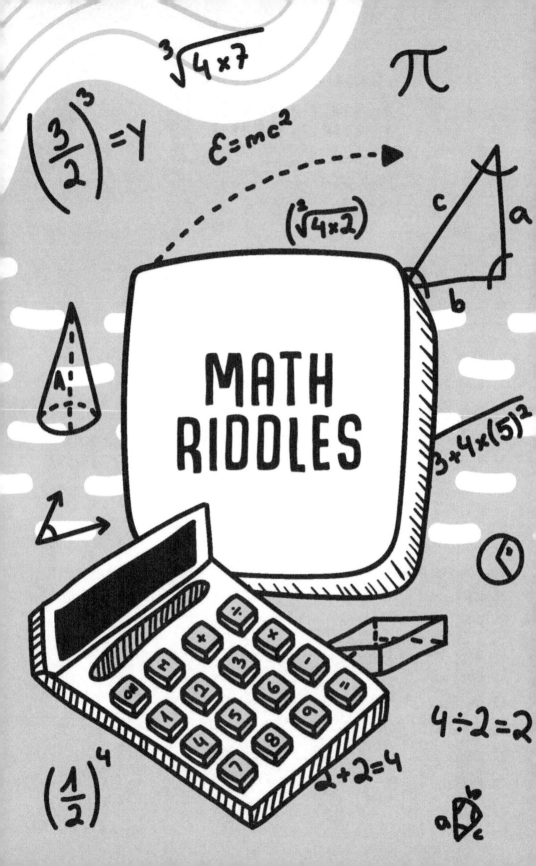

01 If there are three apples and you take away two, *how many do you have?*

02 How many apples grow on trees?

03 What kind of ant is really good at math?

04 I am an odd number. Take away a letter, and I become even. *What number am I?*

05 What number do you get when you multiply all of the numbers on a telephone's number pad?

06 Which weighs more: a pound of feathers, or a pound of bricks?

07 A barrel of water weighs 20 pounds. What must you add to it to make it weigh 12 pounds?

08 If you are in a race and you run past the person in second place, *what place are you in?*

09 How many sides does a circle have?

10 What can you always count on when trying to solve math problems?

11 How many seconds are there in a year?

12 A man is 24 years old but has only had six birthdays. *How is this possible?*

13 There are seven birds on a tree. A hunter shoots one bird down. How many birds are left on the tree?

14 How many birthdays does the average person have?

15 How many bananas can you eat if your stomach is empty?

16 Why is 2+2=5 like your left foot?

17 What do math teachers like to eat?

ANSWERS

1. If you take two apples, then you have two apples.

2. All of them!

3. An accountANT

4. Seven

5. Zero. Anything multiplied by zero will equal zero.

6. Neither. They both weigh one pound.

7. Holes

8. Second place

9. Two — the inside and the outside

10. Your fingers

11. Twelve. January 2nd, February 2nd, March 2nd…

12. He was born on February 29th.

13. None, because the rest of them got scared and flew away.

14. One birthday. The rest are just birthday celebrations or parties.

15. Just one. After that, it's not empty anymore.

16. It's not right.

17. Pi!

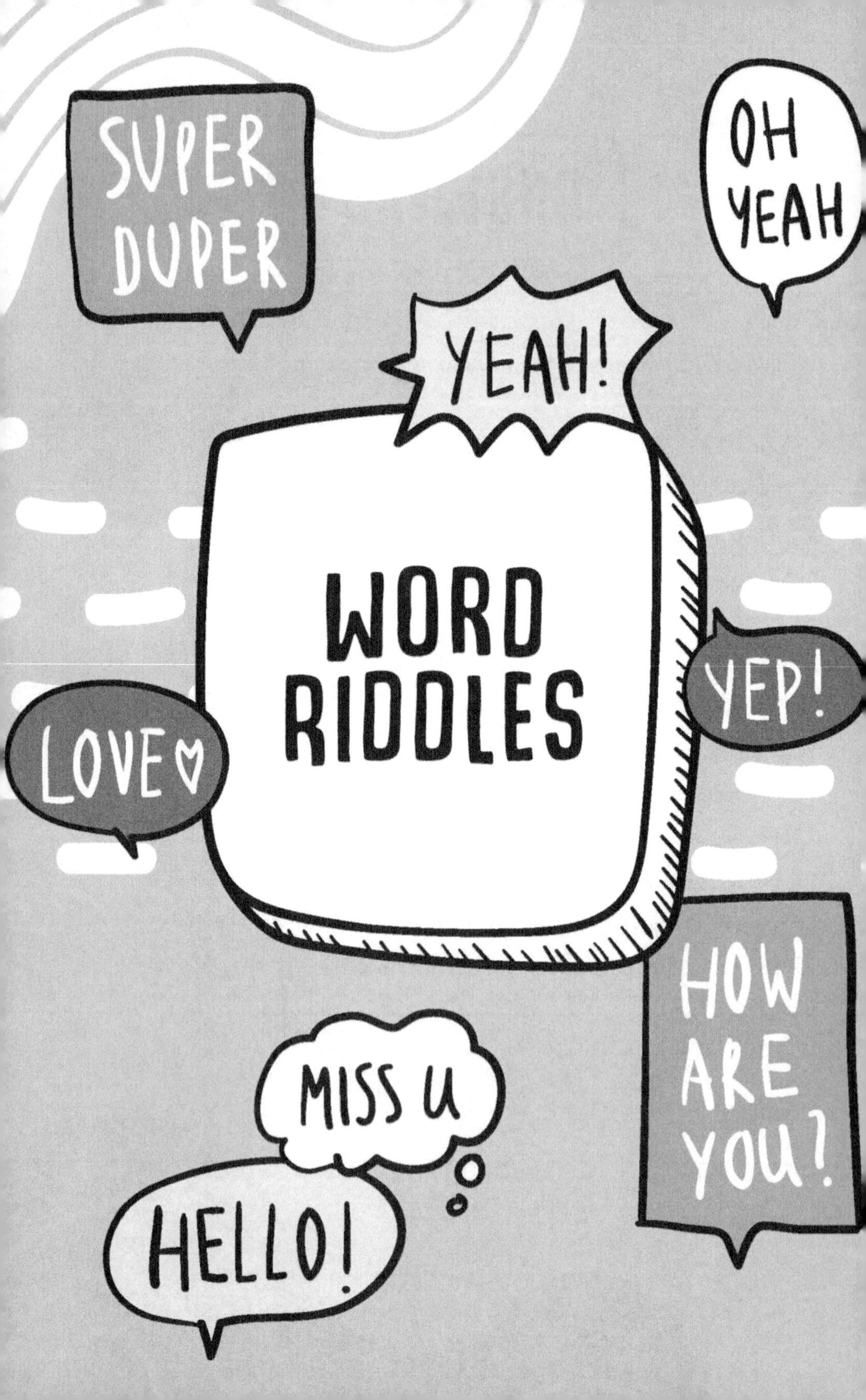
SUPER DUPER
OH YEAH
YEAH!
WORD RIDDLES
YEP!
LOVE
HOW ARE YOU?
MISS U
HELLO!

01 What comes once in a minute, twice in a moment, but never in a thousand years?

02 Where does today come before yesterday?

03 What has three letters and starts with gas?

04 "Angry" and "hungry" are both words that end in -gry. The English language has three words; what is the third word?

05 I am a word of letters three;
Add two, and fewer there will be.
What am I?

06 What is the smartest letter of the alphabet?

07 What word begins and ends with an "E" but only has one letter?

08 What five-letter word becomes shorter when you add two letters to it?

09
I have one, you have one.
If you remove the first letter, a bit remains.
If you remove the second, a bit still remains.
If you remove the third, it still remains.
What is it?

10 What has words but never speaks?

11 What seven-letter word has hundreds of letters in it?

12 Which type of vehicle is spelled the same forwards and backwards?

13 What is in the middle of water but is not an island?

14 When combined, what two words contain the most letters?

15 What three letters change a girl into a woman?

16 Which word contains all 26 letters?

17 What five-letter word has only one left when two letters are removed?

18 I am a word.
If you pronounce me correctly, it will be wrong.
If you pronounce me wrong, it is right.
What word am I?

19 What is the least spoken language in the world?

20 What time of day is spelled the same both forwards and backwards?

21 A word I know, six letters it contains;
Remove one letter, and 12 remain.
What is the word?

22 How do you spell "hard water" with three letters?

23 Take away my first letter, then take away my second letter.
Take away the rest of my letters, yet I remain the same.
What am I?

24 What starts with the letter T, is filled with T, and ends in T?

25 What English word keeps the same pronunciation
even after you take away four of its five letters?

26 What eleven-letter English word is always pronounced incorrectly?

ANSWERS

1. The letter M
2. In the dictionary
3. Cat
4. Language
5. Few
6. The letter A, because it is the highest grade
7. Envelope
8. Short
9. Habit
10. Book
11. Mailbox
12. Racecar
13. T
14. Post office
15. Age
16. Alphabet
17. Stone
18. Wrong
19. Sign language
20. Noon
21. Dozens
22. Ice
23. Postman
24. Teapot
25. Queue
26. Incorrectly

01 You can see me in water, but I never get wet. *What am I?*

02 I'm not alive, but I have five fingers. *What am I?*

03 I have cities, but no houses.
I have mountains, but no trees.
I have water, but no fish.
What am I?

04 You bury me when I'm alive and dig me up when I'm dead. *What am I?*

05 I am pinched by grandmothers. *What am I?*

06 I give milk and I have a horn, but I am not a cow.
What am I?

07 I pass before the sun yet make no shadow.
I can scream and whisper, but I do not speak.
What am I?

08 People need me, but they always give me away. *What am I?*

09 If you drop me, I'll crack,
But if you smile, I'll smile back.
What am I?

10 I travel all over the world but always stay in the same corner. *What am I?*

11 I am full of keys, but I cannot open a single door. *What am I?*

12 I have no life, but I can die. *What am I?*

13 Three eyes have I, all in a row;
When the red one opens, no one can go.
What am I?

14 I only point in one direction, but I guide
people around the world. *What am I?*

15 I have keys but no doors.
I have space but no rooms.
I allow you to enter,
But you are never able to leave.
What am I?

16 Forwards I am heavy, but backwards
I am not. *What am I?*

17 I am often following you and copying your every move.
Yet, you never touch me or catch me.
What am I?

18 If you give me water, I will die. *What am I?*

19 I am tall when I am young and then short when I am old. *What am I?*

20 I have four legs and one back, yet I can't walk. *What am I?*

21 Take off my skin and I won't cry, but you will. *What am I?*

22 I can fly, but I have no wings.
I can cry, but I have no eyes.
Wherever I go, darkness follows me.
What am I?

23 I fly all day long, but don't go anywhere. *What am I?*

24 I am born of water, but when I return to water, I die. *What am I?*

25 I never speak unless spoken to; many have heard me, but none have seen me. *What am I?*

26 I am the only organ in the human body that gave itself its own name. *What am I?*

27 Forwards, I catch fish; backwards, I am the tenth number. *What am I?*

28 I can see when I am with you, but I am blind when alone. *What am I?*

29 I am lighter than air, but a hundred people cannot lift me. Careful, I am fragile. *What am I?*

30

I can be long, or I can be short.
I can be grown, and I can be bought.
I can be round or square.
What am I?

31

In spring, I am full in handsome array;
In summer more clothing I wear.
When colder it grows, I fling off my clothes,
And in winter, quite naked I appear.
What am I?

32

My head is red but turns black when you scratch it. What am I?

33

I am neither a guest, nor a trespasser be.
To this place I belong; it belongs also to me.
What am I?

34

I am the home for feathery animals. What am I?

35

I am a very hot ball up in the sky.
I twinkle and shine, look small and bright.
What am I?

36

I go up, and I go down.
I go towards the sky and towards the ground.
I am present tense and past tense too.
What am I?

37

I have hundreds of legs, but I can only lean.
You make me dirty so you can feel clean.
What am I?

38

I am beautiful, up in the sky.
I am magical, yet I cannot fly.
I am red, blue, purple, and green;
No one can reach me, not even the queen.
To people I bring luck, to some people, riches.
The boy at my end does whatever he wishes.
What am I?

39 I'm ready to walk when I'm all tied up,
But, really, should stop when I'm untied.
What am I?

40 I have a green nose, three red eyes, and four purple ears.
What am I?

41 I'm lighter than what I'm made of,
and more of me is hidden than is seen.
What am I?

42 Take me for a spin, and I'll make you cool,
But use me in the winter, and you are a fool.
What am I?

43 I am milky white, and I scare people. *What am I?*

44 You can drop me from the tallest building and I'll be fine, but if you drop me in water, I die. *What am I?*

45 I have wheels and flies, and yet, I am not an aircraft. *What am I?*

46 I can be entertaining until you realize some pieces of me have been lost. *What am I?*

47 I take off my clothes when you put on your clothes. I put on my clothes when you take off your clothes. *What am I?*

48 Four leaves have I; pick me up, and I will bring you luck. *What am I?*

49

I can fly, but I am not a bird.
I am colorful, but I am not a rainbow.
What am I?

50

I am a fruit, a bird, and also a person.
What am I?

51

I am sometimes powerful, sometimes complex and deep.
I can be blind, lost, or profound.
What am I?

52

I get dirty, I get clean.
I can be delicate but also rough.
People often shake me or smack
me against my own kind.
What am I?

ANSWERS

1. Reflection
2. Glove
3. Map
4. Plant
5. Cheek
6. Milk truck
7. Wind
8. Money
9. Mirror
10. Stamp
11. Piano
12. Battery
13. Traffic light
14. Compass
15. Keyboard
16. Ton
17. Shadow
18. Fire

19. Candle
20. Chair
21. Onion
22. Cloud
23. Flag
24. Ice
25. Echo
26. Brain
27. Net
28. Glasses
29. Bubble
30. Fingernail
31. Tree
32. Match
33. Home
34. Nest
35. Star
36. See-saw

37. Broom
38. Rainbow
39. Shoe
40. Very ugly
41. Iceberg
42. Fan
43. Ghost
44. Paper
45. Garbage truck
46. Puzzle
47. Clothes hanger
48. Shamrock
49. Butterfly
50. Kiwi
51. Love
52. Hands

01 What never asks questions but is often answered?

02 The more you take, the more you leave behind. *What is it?*

03 What is so delicate that saying its name breaks it?

04 What is as light as a feather, but even the world's strongest man couldn't hold it for more than a few minutes?

05 What is given to you and only belongs to you, And yet people use it more than you do?

06 What's full of holes but still holds water?

07 What has one eye but can't see?

08 What has a head and a tail but no body?

09 What is always in front of you but can't be seen?

10 What becomes wetter the more it dries?

11 What can be swallowed but can also swallow you?

12 What has many teeth but can't bite?

13 What comes down but never goes up?

14 What goes through towns and over hills but never moves?

15 What is something you will never see again?

16 What do you throw out when you want to use it but take in when you don't want to use it?

17 Four legs up, four legs down, soft in the middle, hard all around. *What is it?*

18 Man walks over, man walks under; In times of war, he burns asunder. *What is it?*

19 What has six faces but does not wear makeup, has 21 eyes but cannot see?

20 What goes up and down but does not move?

21 What becomes smaller when you turn it upside down?

22 What can fly without wings?

23 What runs all around a backyard yet never moves?

24 What instrument does a skeleton play?

25 What can be picked but not chosen?

26 What do you throw away that keeps returning?

27 What is it that has a bottom at the top of them?

28 What goes up when rain comes down?

29 You wait for it; it cracks, stays for a moment, and then vanishes before your eyes. *What is it?*

30 You can keep it only after giving it away to someone else. *What is it?*

31 If I have it, I don't share it. If I share it, I don't have it. *What is it?*

32 The more you have of it, the less you see. *What is it?*

33 There is an ancient invention still used in some parts of the world today that allows people to see through walls. *What is it?*

34 Poor people have it. Rich people need it. If you eat it, you die. *What is it?*

35 The maker doesn't want it, the buyer doesn't use it, and the user doesn't see it. *What is it?*

36 It has a neck but no head, and it wears a cap. *What is it?*

37 The more there is, the less you see. *What is it?*

38 It's the type of dress that can never be worn. *What is it?*

39
Walk on the living, they don't even mumble.
Walk on the dead, they mutter and grumble.
What are they?

40
What do you serve but never eat?

41
What's got feathers but no wings?

42
What can go through glass without breaking it?

43
What runs and whistles but can't walk or talk?

44
It doesn't bark, it doesn't bite,
but it still won't let you in the house.
What is it?

45 What can you break but not touch?

46 It's been around for a million years, but it's no more than a month old. *What is it?*

47 What has a face and two hands but no arms or legs?

48 What has a lot to say but can't be heard because it can't speak one single word?

49 What can you catch but not throw?

50 What is easy to get into but hard to get out of?

ANSWERS

1. Doorbell
2. Footprints
3. Silence
4. His breath
5. Your name
6. Sponge
7. Needle
8. Coin
9. Future
10. Towel
11. Water
12. Comb
13. Rain
14. Road
15. Yesterday
16. Anchor
17. Bed
18. Bridge
19. Dice
20. Stairs
21. The number nine
22. Time
23. Fence
24. Trombone
25. Nose
26. Boomerang
27. Your legs
28. Umbrella
29. Fireworks
30. Your word
31. Secret
32. Darkness
33. Window
34. Nothing
35. Coffin
36. Bottle
37. Fog
38. Address
39. Leaves
40. Tennis ball
41. Your pillow
42. Light
43. Train
44. Lock
45. Promise
46. The Moon
47. Clock
48. Picture
49. A
50. Trouble

FUNNY
RIDDLES

01 Why did Mickey Mouse go to outer space?

02 What do you call a snowman in the summertime?

03 Why did the smartphone need glasses?

04 Why did the doctor switch jobs?

05 If money really did grow on trees, what would everyone's favorite season be?

06 What is the easiest way to double your money?

07 What was the President's name in 1992?

08 What's the sun's favorite day of the week?

09 What do you call a woman who knows where her husband is all the time?

10 What rooms do ghosts avoid?

11 Did you hear about the soldier who bought a camouflage sleeping bag?

12 Which part of a road do ghosts love to travel the most?

13 What time is it when an elephant sits on your fence?

14 Why can't you trust the law of gravity?

15 How do you make a strawberry shake?

16 What islands should have good singers?

17 Why was the Easter Bunny so upset?

18 Why do French people like to eat snails?

19 Why couldn't the astronaut land on the moon?

20 What did the mother broom say to the baby broom?

21 How do we know that the ocean is friendly?

22 What do you call a witch at a beach?

23 What tire doesn't move when a car turns right?

24 Why is the river rich?

25 Why did the man hold a shoe to his ear?

26 What kind of cup doesn't hold water?

27 What did the baker give his wife for their anniversary?

28 You are in a cold room, and you want to get warm. *How do you get warm?*

29 What kind of tree can you carry in your hand?

30 What kind of bars won't keep a prisoner in jail?

31 What do you call two witches who live together?

32 What is a lifeguard's favorite game?

33 What country would you send a starving man to?

34 Where does one wall meet the other wall?

35 What tastes better than it smells?

36 What ship has two mates but no captain?

37 What has 18 legs and catches flies?

38 What is a mummy's favorite type of music?

39 What is a witch's favorite school subject?

40 Who is the king of all school supplies?

41 What is a cat on ice?

42 What do you get when you cross a chicken and a pig?

43 What age do most travellers have?

44 Why didn't Adam and Eve have a date?

ANSWERS

1. He wanted to visit Pluto.
2. Water
3. It lost all of its contacts.
4. He lost his patients.
5. Fall
6. Put it in front of a mirror.
7. The same as it is today
8. Sunday
9. Widow
10. The living rooms
11. He can't find it.
12. The Dead End
13. Time to get a new fence
14. Because it will always let you down.
15. Tell it a scary story!
16. The Canary Islands
17. He was having a bad hare day.
18. They don't like eating fast food.
19. Because it was full.
20. It's time to go to sweep.
21. It waves.
22. Sandwich
23. The spare tire
24. It has two banks.
25. Because he was listening to sole music.
26. Hiccup
27. Flour
28. Go into the corner. It's always 90 degrees.
29. A palm tree
30. Chocolate bars
31. Broom-mates
32. Pool
33. To Hungary
34. On the corner
35. Your tongue
36. Relationship
37. A baseball team
38. Wrap
39. Spelling
40. The ruler
41. Cool cat
42. Eggs and bacon
43. Baggage
44. They preferred to eat apples, not dates.

01

When it starts to get chilly,
This item is what's chosen
To be wrapped around your neck
So you don't get frozen.
What is it?

02

What has a bed but never sleeps,
Has a mouth, yet never eats?
Always running, never walks,
Often gurgles, never talks?

03

When it's cold in winter,
There is something you love.
It's like tiny white stars
Falling from up above.
What is it?

04

This carries lots of people,
As it's a mode of transport.
You can see a lot of these
If you go to an airport.
What is it?

05

I come in many colors,
And I'm seen on your birthday.
You'd better hold me tightly,
Or else I will float away.
What am I?

06

I'm something that can be pumped
But I am not a tire.
I am a body fluid
That's drunk by a vampire.
What am I?

07

If you want to be a pirate,
You will need this without fail.
So that you can travel around,
You need something you can sail.
What do you need?

08

Of these you will need a pair
If you want to cut some hair.
What are they?

09

I'm a type of public transport
Which follows a certain route.
The wheels on me go round and round;
Of that there should be no doubt.
What am I?

10

Look at the wheels of a car
Or a music CD.
Dartboards, donuts, and most cookies —
This is the shape you see.
What shape is it?

11

I'm sometimes made of fur,
And sometimes made of leather;
I am what you might wear
When outside there's cold weather.
What am I?

12

Usually green, but it can be brown.
It's a great place to play or lie down.
What is it?

13

I am type of toy,
But what kind could I be?
Bratz are one type of brand;
Another is Barbie.
What am I?

14

This is a type of instrument,
But it doesn't require picks
As it doesn't have any strings.
Instead, you play it with some sticks.
What is it?

15

If you were standing still,
And you felt the ground shake,
There's a very good chance
That there was an _____
What happened?

16

It's something that comes in twos;
It's worn on feet and in your shoes.
What is it?

17

In the morning and at night,
A tube of this should be squeezed
So that your teeth can be cleaned
And help keep your parents pleased.
What is it?

18

This is a yellow flower
Which can grow to ten feet tall;
It gives you seeds you can eat
And is turned into oil.
What is it?

19

Here is a riddle about transport,
So it's time to use your brain;
This has an engine and carriages
And runs on rails... it's a _____
What is it?

20

I can be cracked, I can be made.
I can be told, I can be played.
What am I?

21 If there's something high you need to get
But you can't reach it, as you're not tall,
Then you might climb up the rungs of this
After leaning it against a wall.
What is it?

22 You need to press its button
To get to another floor;
However, this thing won't move
Until it has closed its door.
What is it?

23 I'm a type of red card,
But I am not a heart;
Of an engagement ring
I am usually part.
What am I?

24 Never ahead, ever behind, yet flying swiftly past;
For a child it lasts forever. For adults, it's gone too fast.
What is it?

25

Although it's not a curtain,
This gets closed every night
So that you can go to sleep.
It's what gives you your sight.
What is it?

26

You put these on your feet
Whenever you go
To the top of mountains
To slide down the snow.
What are they?

27

People are hired to get rid of me.
I'm often hiding under your bed.
In time I'll always return, you see.
Bite me and you're surely dead.
What am I?

28

With sharp edged wit and pointed poise,
It can settle disputes without making a noise.
What is it?

29 You roll it or you buy it;
People say you shouldn't try it
Because you may get a stroke
From inhaling all that smoke.
What is it?

30 What can you get there in eco-style
Pushed by your legs, mile after mile?

31 What is not a ball
But is a sphere
And holds all lands and people
Year after year?

32 I can be written; I can be spoken.
I can be exposed; I can be broken.
What am I?

33 What has a tongue but cannot talk,
Gets around a lot but cannot walk?

34

It carries paper of the most important sort
But also plastic, I'm glad to report.
What is it?

35

Seven brothers, five work all day;
The other two just play or pray.
What are they?

36

I can bring back the dead and a tear to your eye.
A stir of emotions will follow close by.
What am I?

37

It comes from crystal and melts to a treat.
Add it to your tea to make your tea sweet.
What is it?

38

Forty white horses on a red hill.
They champ, they stamp, and then stand still.
What are they?

39

Fill me up
With hot or cold.
Put anything in me;
I'll make sure I hold.
What am I?

40

This is something with six strings,
And music is what it brings.
What is it?

41

If you are feeling sick,
Get to this building, quick!
What is it?

42

To open a door, you can knock,
Or use this item to unlock.
What is it?

43

This thing can sit two or three
While you all watch TV.
What is it?

44

I can help you see far,
Like the moon or a star.
What am I?

45

The wind and rain
Are my domain.
You might see a twister or two;
Do you feel chilly? I do.
What am I?

46

It is a symphony of noise;
It can produce both grief and joys.
It is inspiring and grand,
Made by a person or a band.
What is it?

47

I am black as night
But can be filled with light.
Through me, things can be seen
Although I am a screen.
What am I?

48
A mysterious, fantastic creature,
It has one defining feature.
And for humans at their worst,
In their eyes it's just a horse.
What is it?

49
My teeth are sharp, my back is straight.
To cut things up is my fate.
What am I?

50
It's shorter than the rest,
But when you are happy,
You raise it up
Like it's the best.
What is it?

51
Brown I am and much admired.
Many horses have I tried;
Tire a horse and worry a man,
Tell me this riddle if you can.
What am I?

52

They try to beat me; they try in vain.
And then I win; I end the pain.
What am I?

53

It can't be seen or felt.
It can't be touched or smelt.
Behind stars and under hills,
All emptiness it fills.
What is it?

54

If you need to draw a circle,
Use a compass to make it great;
And if you need to draw a line,
Use this item to make it straight.
What is it?

55

It doesn't live within a house,
Nor does it live without.
Most will use it when they come in
And again when they go out.
What is it?

56 It keeps you on the ground
And stops things from floating around.
What is it?

57 I live in the corn, and my job is to deter.
Free from pests your crops, I assure.
What am I?

58 I'm named after nothing, though I'm awfully clamorous.
And when I'm not working, your house is less glamorous.
What am I?

59 Round as an apple, deep as a cup,
And all the kings' horses can't fill it up.
What is it?

60 More rare today than long ago,
There's a salutation from friends written below.
What is it?

61

A mile from end to end,
Yet as close to as a friend.
A precious commodity, freely given.
Seen on the dead and on the living.
Found on the rich, poor, short and tall,
But shared among children most of all.
What is it?

62

Its tail is round and hollow,
It seems to get chewed a bit,
But you'll rarely see this thing
Unless the other end is lit.
What is it?

63

I love to dance and twist and prance;
I shake my tail as away I sail.
Wingless, I fly into the sky.
What am I?

64

One simple click, one simple flash.
Preserving a memory, for years I will last.
What am I?

ANSWERS

1. Scarf
2. River
3. Snow
4. Airplane
5. Balloon
6. Blood
7. Boat
8. Scissors
9. Bus
10. Circle
11. Coat
12. Grass
13. Doll
14. A drum
15. Earthquake
16. Socks
17. Toothpaste
18. Sunflower
19. Train
20. Joke
21. Ladder
22. Elevator

23. Diamond
24. Childhood
25. Eye
26. Skis
27. Dust
28. Sword
29. Cigarette
30. Bicycle
31. Earth
32. News
33. Shoe
34. Wallet
35. Week
36. Memories
37. Sugar
38. Teeth
39. Cup
40. Guitar
41. Hospital
42. Key
43. Sofa
44. Telescope

45. Weather
46. Music
47. Television
48. Unicorn
49. Saw
50. Thumb
51. Saddle
52. Death
53. Space
54. Ruler
55. Door
56. Gravity
57. Scarecrow
58. Vacuum cleaner
59. Well
60. Letter
61. Smile
62. Pipe
63. Kite
64. Photograph

01 What is a father's child and a mother's child, yet no one's son?

02 What goes up and down but never moves?

03 It is where kings, queens, knights, and bishops go to war together. *What is it?*

04 Mr. Blue lives in the blue house. Mr. Yellow lives in the yellow house, and Mr. Black lives in the black house. *Who lives in the white house?*

05 Besides Paris, what is the capital of France?

06 Snow White was friendly with seven of them.

07 Where do you find an ocean with no water?

08 What is at the end of a rainbow?

09 What gives you strength and power to walk through walls?

10 How many people are dead in an average graveyard?

11 Where is the ocean deepest?

12 When is homework not homework?

13 How do snails travel?

14 My girlfriend wears this on her body, eyes, lips and face.
What is it?

15 Without this, everyone would lose their head.
What is it?

16 What is the first thing a gardener plants in the garden?

17 What is between heaven and Earth?

18 What is taken before you get it?

19 You answer me, although I never ask you questions.
What am I?

20 I am a tree with five branches, no leaves, and no fruit.
What am I?

21 Poorly behaved children often find themselves sitting in these.

22 I have a thousand wheels, but move I do not.
Call me what I am, call me a lot.
What am I?

23 To cross the water, I'm the way.
For water I'm above; I touch it not.
And truth to say, I neither swim nor move.
What am I?

ANSWERS

1. Daughter
2. Temperature
3. Chess
4. The President
5. "F"
6. Dwarfs
7. On a map
8. "W"
9. Doors
10. All of them.
11. At the bottom.
12. When you do it in class

13. Slowly
14. Makeup
15. Neck
16. Foot
17. "And"
18. Your picture
19. Telephone
20. Arm
21. Corners
22. Parking lot
23. Bridge

01 What can you share and still have all for yourself?

02 Name three consecutive days without saying Wednesday, Friday, and Sunday.

03 How can a man go for 20 days without sleeping?

04 The more you look at it, the less you see. *What is it?*

05 Who are people you see every day but you don't know?

06 You are my brother, but I am not your brother. *Who am I?*

07

I get filled with water, but I'm not a drinking glass.
I spin, but I'm not a propeller.
I clean things, but I'm not a janitor.
I'm a household appliance, but I'm not a dishwasher.
I have clothes put in me, but I'm not a closet.
What am I?

08

I have seats, but I'm not a classroom.
I have mirrors, but I'm not a barber shop.
I have windows, but I'm not a room.
I have wheels, but I am not an airplane.
I have a trunk, but I'm not an elephant.
What am I?

09

What can hold all days, weeks, and months but still fit on a table?

10

What is a deep well full of knives?

11

What is found over your head but under your hat?

12 Born in a shell, I adorn your neck.
What am I?

13 What is all over a house?

14 Who plays when he works and works when he plays?

15 If you're worried that grandpa will bite, just remove these.

16 What do people make that you can't see?

17 What is black and white and red all over?

18 What's higher than the king?

19 I am nothing but holes tied to holes, yet I am strong as iron. *What am I?*

20 I have many feathers to help me fly.
I have a body and head, but I'm not alive.
It is your strength that determines how far I go.
You can hold me in your hand, but I'm never thrown.
What am I?

21 What is common to eat before it's born and after it's dead?

22 I am but three holes. When you come out of me, you are still inside me. *What am I?*

23 What stays on the ground but never gets dirty?

24 Who makes moves while remaining seated?

ANSWERS

1. Knowledge
2. Yesterday, today, and tomorrow
3. He sleeps at night.
4. Sun
5. Strangers
6. Your sister
7. Washing machine
8. Car
9. Calendar
10. Mouth
11. Hair
12. Pearl
13. Roof
14. Actor
15. Dentures
16. Noise
17. Newspaper
18. Crown
19. Chain
20. Arrow
21. Egg
22. Shirt
23. Shadow
24. A chess player

01 What makes you young?

02 If your aunt's brother is not your uncle, what relation is he to you?

03 If you jump off the top of a building, where do you land?

04 What do you have after you take away the whole but some still remains?

05 How do you make "one" disappear?

06 What is the difference between the North Pole and the South Pole?

07 What kind of a coat can only be put on if it's wet?

08 What loses a head in the morning but gains a head at night?

09 What falls but does not break, and what breaks but does not fall?

10 What walks on four feet in the morning, two in the afternoon, and three at night?

11 Beth's mother has three daughters. One is called Laura, the other one is Sarah. What is the name of the third daughter?

12 Who can shave 25 times a day but still have a beard?

13 What does almost no one want to have, yet almost no one wants to lose?

14 What can you hold in your left hand but not in your right?

15 What is cut on a table but is never eaten?

16 What stays where it is even after it goes off?

17 What travels from coast to coast without ever moving?

18 There is a kind of fish that can never swim.
What is that?

19 What breaks on the water but never on the land?

20 What has four eyes but can't see?

21 You will always find me in the past.
I can be created in the present,
but the future can never taint me.

22 What is it that, if you are given
one, you'll have either two or none?

23 How does a dog cross a river without getting wet?

24 I have no wings but I fly;
I have no teeth but I bite.
What am I?

25 What's the last thing people want on their hands?

26
I dig out tiny caves and store gold and silver in them.
I also build bridges of silver and make crowns of gold.
If you are in pain, you need my help,
Yet many are afraid to let me help them.
What am I?

27
I work hard almost every day —
not much time to dance and play.
I do all that for you in good health to stay.
What am I?

28
We hurt without moving.
We poison without touching.
We bear the truth and the lies.
We are not to be judged by our size.
What are we?

29

No thicker than your finger when it folds.
As thick as what it's holding when it holds.
What is it?

30

Passed from father to son and
shared between brothers,
Its importance is unquestioned,
though it is used more by others.
What is it?

ANSWERS

1. Adding the letters "ng"

2. He is your father.

3. In the hospital

4. Wholesome

5. Add a "g," and it's "gone."

6. All the difference in the world

7. A coat of paint

8. A pillow

9. Night and day

10. Man. When he is a child, he crawls on all fours; when he is older, he walks on two legs, and when he is old-aged, he uses a cane.

11. Beth

12. A barber

13. Their job

14. Your right elbow

15. A deck of cards

16. An alarm clock

17. Highway

18. Dead fish

19. A wave

20. Mississippi

21. History

22. Choice

23. The river is frozen.

24. Bullet

25. Handcuffs

26. Dentist

27. Doctor

28. Words

29. A paper bag

30. Surname

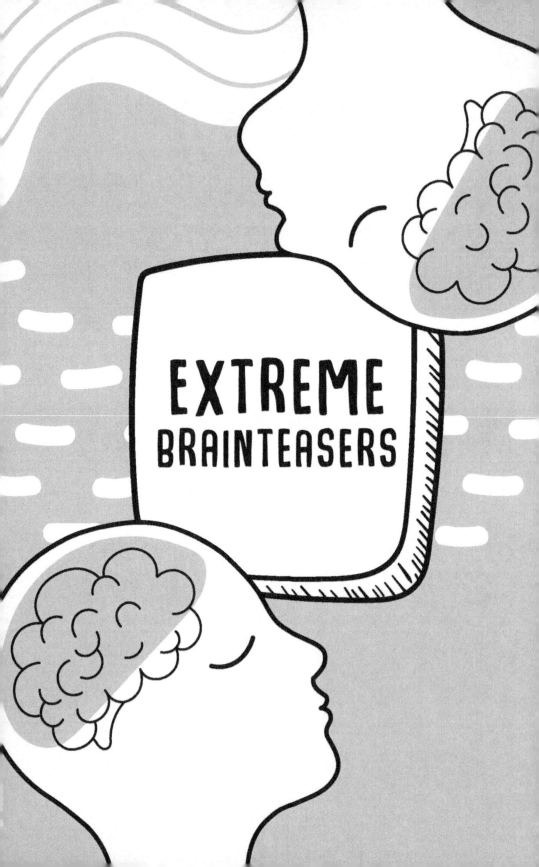

01 How far can a dog run into the woods?

02 If three dogs and one cat weren't standing under an umbrella, how did none of them get wet?

03 How many animals did Moses bring on the ark?

04 What question can you never answer "yes" to?

05 The last man on Earth received a phone call from someone; *who was the caller?*

06 What is the difference between a jeweler and a jailer?

07 He has married many women but has never been married. *Who is he?*

08 What question can someone ask all day long, always get completely different answers, and yet all the answers could be correct?

09 If you drop soap on the floor, is the floor clean or the soap dirty?

10 You walk across a bridge and you see a boat full of people, yet there isn't a single person on board. *How is that possible?*

11 When you look for something, why is it always in the very last place you look?

12 Two men are in a desert. They both have packs on. One of the guys is dead. The guy who is alive has his pack open, the guy who is dead has his pack closed. *What is in the pack?*

13 If a doctor gives you three pills and tells you to take one pill every half hour, how long would it take before all the pills had been taken?

14 Imagine you're in a room that is filling up with water. There are no windows or doors. *How do you get out?*

15 You draw a line. Without touching it, how do you make the line longer?

16 How can you throw a ball as hard as you can to only have it come back to you, even if it doesn't bounce off anything?

17 If an electric train is going east at 60 miles per hour and there is a strong westerly wind, which way does the smoke from the train drift?

18 If a red house is made of red bricks, and a yellow house is made of yellow bricks, what is a greenhouse made of?

19 Why can't a man living in New York be buried in Chicago?

20 A man walked through the rain for an hour without getting a single hair on his head wet. He didn't have an umbrella, he wasn't wearing a hat, and he didn't have anything to hold over his head. How could it be that not a single hair on his head got wet?

21 Before Mount Everest was discovered, what was the highest mountain in the world?

22 A king, a queen, and two twins all lay in a large room, yet there are no adults or children in the room. *How is that possible?*

23 A pipe, a carrot, and a couple of sticks are lying together in a field. *Why?*

24 You live in a one-story building made entirely of redwood. What color would the stairs be?

25 Do other countries besides America have the 4th of July?

26 You have a single match and are in a pitch-black room with a candle, an oil lamp, and a gas stove. Which do you light first?

27 On Christmas Eve, when Santa leaves his workshop at the North Pole, what direction does he travel?

28 What happens after it rains cats and dogs?

29 A plane crashes between the border of Canada and America. Where do you bury the survivors?

30 A boy fell off a 20-foot ladder and yet wasn't hurt. *Why not?*

31 If a rooster laid a brown egg and a white egg, what kind of chicks would hatch?

32 What are you certain to find inside your pocket when you reach into it?

33 There is a man in a four-story building. He jumps out of the window and is unharmed. He used no padding, yet he wasn't injured. *How is this possible?*

34 If two is a company and three is a crowd, what are four and five?

1. The dog can run into the woods only halfway; if it ran any further, it would run out of the woods!

2. It wasn't raining!

3. Moses didn't bring anything on the ark; Noah did.

4. "Are you asleep?"

5. A woman

6. A jeweler sells watches, and a jailer watches cells.

7. A priest

8. "What time is it?"

9. It depends on the floor.

10. All the people on the boat are married.

11. Because that's when you stop looking.

12. A parachute

13. An hour. Take the first pill right away; half an hour later, take the second; and half an hour after, take the third pill.

14. Stop imagining!

15. You draw a shorter line next to it, and it becomes the longer line.

16. Throw the ball straight up in the air.

17. Smoke doesn't come from electric trains.

18. Glass; all greenhouses are made of glass.

19. Because he is alive.

20. He didn't have any; he was bald.

21. Mount Everest. It was always the highest, even before it was discovered.

22. They are all beds.

23. They're what is left of a melted snowman.

24. What stairs? You live in a one-story house.

25. Yes; they also have the 5th and 6th of July...

26. The match

27. South. If you are at the North Pole, the only direction you can go is south.

28. You step in a poodle.

29. They are survivors — you don't bury them.

30. He fell off the bottom step.

31. None. Roosters don't lay eggs.

32. Your hand

33. He jumped out of the ground floor.

34. Nine

FINAL WORDS

Thank you so much for taking the time
to read my book!

I hope you enjoyed reading these amazing
riddles as much as I enjoyed writing them
(which I can assure you, was a whole lot).

Now, the best thing about this huge book of
riddles is that it never truly ends. I mean,
you have this book forever, which means you
can share these great riddles with your friends
and family time and time again.

So, what are you waiting for?

Get reading, get sharing—and most importantly,
get riddling!

Printed in Great Britain
by Amazon

10326097R00066